THE ALTAR OF AMAZING CHANCE

THE ALTAR OF AMAZING CHANCE

Dear Marie –
Thank you for
your friendship –
you are an amazing spirit!

poems by

Margot Lavoie

Margot Lavoie
8/09

Two Poets Ink
Fayetteville

ISBN-10: 0-9841314-1-8
ISBN-13: 978-0-9841314-1-9

13 12 11 10 09 5 4 3 2 1

Editor: Mendy Knott
Book Design: Liz Lester Design (www.lizlesterdesign.com)
Cover art: Ginny Masullo

Two Poets INK
An Imprint of Limbertwig Press
15048 Draper Road, Fayetteville, Arkansas 72704-0302
(479) 582-1092
www.twopoets.us

For Tom, Beth, Trevor and Sarah

With love—
because *Borta bra, men hemma bäst*

(*Away is good, but home is best*—SWEDISH PROVERB)

CONTENTS

BORTA
(away)

HEMMA
(home)

Dear Reader,

Most of the pieces in this collection are drawn from my family life, my experiences with the natural world and my travels. As an organizing principle I have chosen a favorite Swedish proverb, *Borta bra, men hemma bäst*—away is good, but home is best—because, although my family is not Swedish, my mother had a beautiful ceramic tile hanging in her kitchen with this saying. Today I have the same tile hanging in my own kitchen, reminding me that while travel is truly wonderful, that sense of coming home at last is always very sweet. May these poems let you wander, then bring you home again.

Margot Lavoie

BORTA

(away)

deviation

escape is a matter of time
time is a method of waiting
waiting is a condition of life
unless you taste impatience
like sea salt on your tongue
and tack off against the wind
on some crazy tangent
whenever a blue moon rises
and you don't care anymore
where your next meal comes from
or if you make landfall
by morning

chinook

last night
dreaming
I migrated north
with Canadian geese

we flew high
and in darkness
avoiding the false stars below
that clustered to misguide us

each day
water in the ponds
grew colder
until home at last
we slept weary on ice

in the morning
I awoke
my arms heavy
and aching
as I lifted the window open
to the first warm breeze
of spring

entering Truro

each summer
we migrate to the coast
like clockwork
as though drawn back
to some birthing ground
by instinct alone

we fight our way
through heavy traffic
along the arm Cape Cod throws
out into the sea
entering Truro at last
somewhere near the wrist
where our beach is waiting

with that first glimpse of ocean
that first sound of waves
everything else drifts away
beyond the horizon
and all I want to do
is drink this place down
in huge gulps of sky and sea
and light until the colors
run down my chin
and my blood turns salty

until I grow seaweed for hair
and my skin pebbles smooth

in the roll of the tide
I want to keep drinking and drinking
this landscape down
until Truro enters
the last outpost of my body
ready to stand guard there
and in the darkest days of winter
throw out a lifeline
to save my sanity

landlocked

behind my eyes
these rolling fields
are breakers coming in

here in the heart
of hill and prairie
so far from any shore

my uncertain moon
still wanders
a prisoner of tides

that draw out tears
like rain falling finally
at the end of a dry season

when each cloud flowing
over the hot horizon
seems so like the dove

returned at last
with green life
to tell the story of land

yet in this state
all I can see
is water

coyotes

once
near a darkening stretch
of Cape Cod beach
we caught the glow
of their small moon eyes
luminescent in the scrub
at the edge of the parking lot
a pair standing silently
watching us watch them
then moving off abruptly
across the dunes

later
by the side
of an Adirondack road
we drove past a lone prowler
stalking the sunset
on those incredibly delicate legs
the huge tail a creature
almost of itself
vanishing with its owner
into the woods

last night
sleepless past two
I heard the tremolo lifting
the yip yip of a pack running
through the neighbor's pasture

his cattle calling out
their anguish to the wind
startled like me by this wildness
so close to home
the remembered taste of blood
bitter now
inside their tender mouths

old clans

quick tears well up
on the way to work
early enough to beat the buses
driving into the sun just rising now
revealing the night's small tragedies
on this two lane slaughterhouse
that silences both the domestic
and the wild

two victims this morning
laid out on the shoulders
face each other across the road
large black dog on the left
with hints of lab mix collie
long hair white vest and socks
mouth open legs stretched still
running through the last dream

tabby cat on the right
turned to meet the opponent
back arched fur bristled
legs splayed out stiff
grown tired of the chase
ready for battle at last

they were martyrs
for the honor of old clans
canine and feline to the end

blinded by their animosity
to the swift approach of death
through the cold indifference of steel
crushing their bodies in surprise
the last breath exhaled out
in whispered prayers
to their separate cruel
and most unyielding
gods

half-mast

these days
the cup is half empty
not full
painful plans are made
and hopes abandoned

these days
we are shown portraits
but not of the living
we hear radio biographies
on our morning commute
and arrive at work weeping
over gardens no longer tended
dreams made impossible
poems never written

these days
the flag flies half-mast
too often
in that semaphore for sorrow
totem carved from cloth and wind
raised up to speak
our lineage of loss

in these days
these dark
and darkening
days

winter coming on

in the cathedral of autumn
the trees ignite
small bonfires of joy
under a stratus cloud vault
of pewter

I come here
to place a candle
on this altar of light
but find no saints or relics
only an aging woman
reflected in the font

her head silvered
by an early frost
with winter coming on
hair and leaves
true colors revealed
as the secret engines of life
start shutting down

and time flows away
faster than smoke
rising into November's cold
faster than flocked birds

rising in a rush of wings
dark against the sky

the sudden explosion of life
holding beautiful and holy
for this moment
then gone

star songs

Piazzolla is tangoing
from the car radio
under a forever see
seeming sky
of blackening silk
clear November night
filigreed with seed pearl
and sequined stars

remembering
under such pure history
of light years gone
the midnight bowl
of an Adirondack lake
pulsing with reflected jewels
marking the warrior's way
to heaven

remembering
the cold sand blanket
of a Cape Cod beach
spread beneath our backs
as we watched for meteors
quick silvered fireflies
falling faster and faster
towards dawn

remembering
all the wishes made then
all the forgotten songs

deer crossings

you see them
in the most unlikely places
lying with legs splayed out
neck flung back
mouth open in surprise
at the sudden departure
of the last breath

they are there
on the interstate shoulder
no more than a mile
from center city
there beneath the railroad overpass
down by the river
and once even
on the access road
that enters the mall

they have passed through
the final intersection
on that road map of misfortune
we drew through their country
long ago
our hard dark scars
cutting the tender skin
of their world

but now they rise up
like mist along a highway
as though to warn us
we will come to that same crossing
the universe of random chance
patterning our landscape
no differently from theirs

the border

in late July
we are swimming the Buffalo
just east of the Jasper bridge
where the river slows its run
into clear deep pools
and you can wash away
the heat of town
plunging over and over
through shafts of liquid sunlight

resting in the shallows
we anchor ourselves
on time-worn gravel
to float suspended above
the incredible whiteness of our hands
while this year's delicate hatchlings
slowly gather around our arms

their silvered silk ribbon bodies
pause and undulate
as though amazed
to find what might be slivers
of the pale summer moon
fallen down into their home
as we are amazed
by the simple joy of this watching
here on the border
between the world of water
and the world of air

seeing the city

in Albany
an early spring rain
falls on the bronze horseman
poised at the Capitol steps
while the park grass greens
but the trees still wait naked
for the sun to dress them
they stand up stiff
revealing all their secrets
with last year's empty nests

today I should revel in my freedom
but instead I walk this city
looking for my son
no longer the child
who with a bird's eye view
drew downtown streets
from far above
now he is apprentice
to all the master builders
who have gone before
and stays locked in his studio
a clubhouse that mothers may not enter

but on these streets today
he can come walking with me
when I see the city
through his eyes
the ornamental iron across an alley

down near Beaver Street
the lattice of stone and steel and glass
along the Hudson
and St. Peter's spire sailing
above the row houses
looking up from Pine

walking and walking
until we find the city's heart
then lean back to look together
and breathe out a long essential sigh
now that is sweet

seasons imagined for a flat land

winter

simplest of seasons
the land carries little now
but the wind's light vessel
and a brooding silence
as water waits for storm

spring

birthing undercurrents everywhere
turbulence thrusts up from the darkness
into cacophonies of song that rise
to follow the great ship of the living
safely back to port

summer

nothing is concealed now
at noon no shadow but your own
and the skimming clouds' dark hulls
pulling all your expectations away
in their wake

autumn

this once sea still stretches
the soul's eye beyond the horizon
turning tides by that raw wind kicked up
down the dirt road forevers of life

imperceptible undulations of browning grass
and hard-packed ground breaking in waves

breaking in waves that rise then release
all these burdens I have carried
scattering now across the plain
in some cartography of flotsam
strange map of my former life

scattering now as chart points
laid down at random
to compass a way
from all these longings
I no longer desire

strange comfort

on the high wire
that curves along Double Springs Road
the owl perched motionless
facing west

just past seven
on the morning rush to work
the bird was there suddenly
around a bend of mist
a tawny feathered jewel
set so surprisingly in this ordinary day

leaving me to wonder
why had it lingered into the dawn
but understanding only it was a talisman
waiting on the portal to that other world
that goes on living
despite our daily lives

that other world
where deer go on running through the pasture
despite the fence's vigilance
and coyotes call out the night
despite the candle's flame

yet always
there comes strange comfort
in that calling

living outside the box

all over the country
old barns are collapsing
their hapless inhabitants abruptly evicted
take up residence in nearby homes

suddenly
there are bats roosting in the attic
making their presence known
by a sound or an odor
becoming a nuisance
an irrational fear in the dark
becoming something that something
must be done about

so we build them boxes
lure them out to the periphery
far from the circles of our daily life
and most seem satisfied
boxes being perhaps better
than barns

but just a few
having had enough of civilization all together
strip off epochs of evolution
like layers of clothing on a warm winter day
and head out
across the flat landscape of mankind
falling off the edge into memory
of damp stone and caves

at twilight
their fragile bodies fill and tremble
with the ancient songs
now homeless by choice
they live in the garden of their desire
beyond our dominion
feral and free again

hurricane door

time comes
when you must step off the train
that has been your life
you closed your eyes once
in the sleeping car
and forty years were gone

now
place your feet firmly on the platform
make at least this gesture
this first step
into that hard wind
always blowing across the world
blowing everything you once recognized
gone

until what seems so solid
turns to smoke
what seems permanent
turns temporary
then vanishes

leaving you with nothing
but to pass clean through this station
without luggage
or the clothing of years

leaving you with nothing
but to start again
find a boat perhaps
float out over the shallows
and straight through some hurricane door
strange gate blown open
caught in a mangrove sieve

lost remnant of what once was
turned portal now
and change
your only ticket

poetry on the interstate

with thanks to Robert Bly

be very careful
if you listen to poetry
alone on the interstate
have lots of gas
you may go past your destination
forgetting yourself and where you're going
a temporary missing person

don't stop for food
you will not eat it
but you will be very thirsty

don't go too fast
slow down
or the poetry police
will pull you over

you will pass
through a foreign landscape
even though you've been there
many times before
the road will become
the back of someone else's hand

but if the trip is hard
a lover left behind
out of some cold necessity
and not by your design
the poet's voice will carry you
without any effort at all
until suddenly you awake
to find your journey done

road work

bulldozers are bringing down buildings
along the road I travel each day
where the slow stream of traffic
has turned into a flood
overflowing the narrow banks
of this one lane river

one by one the landmarks are falling
leaving no means to plot my course
no stars left to fix in the sextant
of peripheral vision

first the dairy bar
where buses and trucks
had always been welcome
"please park in back"
next the convenience mart
reduced to rubble in a single day
only the long line of silver coolers
left standing
then the lawn and garden supply
and finally the local tavern
where happy hour is now
most certainly over

one by one
they are sinking back
into a featureless landscape
fading from memory
through a rare and progressive amnesia
that slowly erases my life

until I understand
the meaning of mementos
the importance of keepsakes
why we always go back into the burning house
to save that one old photograph

now all these journeys
seem only imagined
as though I had never
really been here
at all

HEMMA

(home)

the altar of amazing chance

sunlight glanced off rolling mower blades
moving through the hayfield towards the boy
waiting nearly invisible inside a forest of stems
waiting to call to his father
the father who did not see the son
until the sound of metal cutting down to bone

the father who did not see the son
until the grass was screaming
the whole world screaming
as he stumbled across the fields
the boy leaving in his arms
a dark river of blood behind them

the father who ran screaming across the
barnyard
and the hired hands working in the silo
dropped their tools and ran

the father who ran screaming across the lawn
and the boy's mother working in the garden
dropped her bowl and ran

the father who ran screaming into the kitchen
laying the boy quiet now on the table
a crimson flood beneath him
when the bleeding would not stop
just would not stop

until a young man
come to help with the harvest
tied off the wound
and with an apron string
let my father live

in the luck of that one moment
my own history was born
leading me here now
one more pilgrim dancing ecstatic
on the altar of amazing chance

gathering darkness

now is the time of letting go
the old year sent at last
to gathering darkness

darkness
so seductive a lover
arms opened wide
until consumed
you fall in

now is the time of giving away
stripping down to the bare essence
of what is needed
as winter strips the land bare
of the living

through the long night
you learn
as the Shakers learned
to love the fierce beauty
inside emptiness

emptiness that scours clean
the vessel of your life
until
when the seasons turn
you are ready
to take communion
from the golden body
that is light

inch worm

somewhere west of Terre Haute
my husband is driving towards the sunset
flowing with the traffic down Highway 70
my sweet pioneer
starting all over again

tomorrow in Arkansas
he'll be unpacking
as I pack things away
filling up closets
as I empty others out
studying new maps
as I discard the old

we've danced
this pas de deux before
his actions
the mirror image of mine
as we move forward
into the future
like the inch worm

first he releases
stretches out
then grabs on tight again
as I prepare
to let the past go
release and follow

the long slender body
of our history
our love
holding us fast
a tender tether of longing
running from one
to the other

the guest towels

remembering Grandma's house
where I spent one month each summer
I see embroidered guest towels
arranged carefully on an ornate bar
she had made them years ago
when threading a needle was still possible
when delicate stitching did not strain the eyes

one towel for each week day
with a young woman in Victorian dress
washing on Monday
baking on Tuesday
happily working her way
to that Sunday stroll to church

my dolls and I would play 'old-fashioned'
would follow the towel routine
imagining this was how Grandma used to live

until I realized the towel lady
had never really lived there
had never lost her husband
widowed at twenty four
with two small boys to raise
never pawned her wedding gifts for food
or kissed her sons goodbye together gone to war
content in her idyllic landscape
the towel lady had never ventured
into Grandma's harsh terrain

but ever the optimist
Grandma would tell me of the simple joys
that dreams were free and hope was always there
if only you had a talisman to find it

it was there in the pasture flowers
held in an old mason jar
there on your tongue
with the first sweet grapes of summer
and there in a line of lovely linen towels
that held our yearning
for a simpler and more perfect world

playing house

among crock pot cookers
we stew uncertainly
daughter and I
one unit in eight
with four square rooms
at least there's space
to hang out
my Maxfield Parrish blues
as Arlo sings "Oh come on"
and I wonder what
am I coming to

naming Bethsheba

bionic baby
brownie pledger
book worm
brother baiter
born slob
belly acher
brain brat
bareback rider
boy dater
bar hopper
blue bitch
BYE FOREVER
been there done that
back later
bone shaker
bet taker
barn raiser
boat rocker
beans not bombs
bran baker
Benning to Baghdad
ban breaker
best friend
beautiful dreamer
Bethsheba
better world maker

addiction

on a drizzly February evening
just a few parking spots down
from where we pulled in
a car door opens

revealing the quick surprise
of black stockings in stylish heels
below a very short skirt
dressed to the nines she is
and tall

without thinking
you draw your breath in fast
at this unexpected glimpse of desire
here in the drab winter dark

and suddenly I remember
you once told me that perhaps
it was my own black stockings
that led from one thing to another
all those years ago

and then I remember that perhaps
it was your fisherman's knit sweater
how jeans molded softly
down the long beauty of your legs
or the heady fragrance of your skin

of your very being
that first drew me in

drew me in so deep
to this sweet addiction
that decades later it still lingers
rich and smoky on my soul

watching my son as he draws

twenty years have come and gone
yet I can still remember
the perfection of your hands

unfolding like tender buds
on that first day long ago
when they laid you beside me

the blueprint for my new life
drawn inside your tiny palms

at the 30th Street station

for Sarah

we stand waiting
by the angel of journeys
that graceful totem rising above the lobby
where travelers pause to whisper up
their secret prayers

here in this house of possibility
chance is laboring everyday
on the delicate edifice of the now
and we all arrive in anticipation
with our blueprints for change
rolled up carefully under our arms

when the time comes we hold up our plans
for the architecture of this moment
printed with the names of the never met
wondering if this was how you spell future
wondering if a new room would be added
to that intricate house of lives

all those lives
that form the invisible scaffolding
on which the present stands

all those lives
crossing and re-crossing
merging and bending away through time
like the trains that are passing now
through the darkness
beneath our feet

September passage

before work I sit in my car
remembering another September morning
when the Wisconsin air was moist
with a harbor freshness as though
the ocean had traveled inland overnight
to cover our prairie town

remembering being up all night
unable to rest and floundering
out among those rhythmic waves
that came faster and stronger
near dawn

remembering the ride to the hospital
nervous as a sailor with strange clouds ahead
that could not be understood or avoided
knowing the sea was about to change
forever

now
years later
though you won't admit it
you are nervous too
starting your own passage to a new world
while I must be content to stand on the
breakwater
straining for that last glimpse
as you drift out and away
beyond land's end

the way he rolls

it's the way he rolls in bed
like the ocean at high tide
breaking across the sandbar of my body
then dragging off the blankets inch by inch
and pulling them out to sea
leaving me nearly naked by dawn
when I wake in the early morning chill
to the soft steady rhythm of his breathing
that always reminds me
how much I love the sound
of the waves as they come rolling
rolling in

March madness

start living life
in different ways

discard old patterns
from your past

eat salad for breakfast
cold cereal at night

lie down on the rug
and roll with the cat

empty closets and secrets
then turn all the beds

make wild love in the morning
this season won't last

the smelt run

all night we kept the fire burning
with driftwood and debris
anything we could find
along this rocky shelf
that called itself a beach
east shore Ontario
the smelt running

we stayed past dawn
past parental curfews
past the serious fishermen
working slowly through the shallows
as the hours of that night
flowed sweet and easy
with cigarettes and beer
around those smoky flames
until the sun broke low
behind the pale dunes

years later
my daughter's own wild nights
were dark and wilder still
hanging on the ragged edge
of some unknowable abyss
until the bargain struck
and her promise kept
she left for another state

I carried her new life
up old tenement stairs
the final door shutting
my presence now intolerable
for one moment more

then drove home alone
on the turnpike heading west
with her words so sharp
yet once my own
catching in my throat
like small fish bones

the geography of passion

there is a hillside
near our home
that curves along the horizon
like the line my hand
draws along your body
from shoulder to thigh
in the morning after love

on the hill crest
a tree row marks the border
between two farms
graceful sentinels on duty
in all types of weather
the light held in their branches
stars in a net

sometimes in the spring
mist rises after rain
wrapping the trees in gauze
diffuse and ephemeral
softening the geography
as the years have softened
our time together

but in the autumn light pours down
with such fire on the hill
it seems as though the sun itself
has fallen
passing through the ground
without a trace

as St. Teresa's arrow might fall
searing through my heart over and over
annealing the body of my soul
with your passion

when the heat breaks

the temperature builds all day long
piling cumulus clouds up above the horizon
their weight pressing the land still
flat and silent

until just after sunset
a cool breeze picks up
and skirts along our front porch
drawing a few low notes from the wind chime
before it snakes away through the long grass
in the neighbor's hayfield

giving the crickets back their voice
beginning the music of this summer evening
the chorus rising with peepers and cicadas
as the world revives

with so much life
even the stones
start singing

the joy that works the body

Arkansas August sizzles
Sunday into triple digits
on the time temperature display
at the center of town
as life boils down to a silent simmer
just holding its breath for fall

inside our cool cocoon house
we move quietly through the hottest hours
only emerging in late afternoon
to head for the local pool

there everyone under twenty
is queuing for the board
while we drift in the relative freedom
of the deep end

half asleep
from a lazy back float
near the diving zone rope
I watch the cannonballs and belly flops
fly up over my toes and vanish

until one slender summer-skinned boy
caught somewhere between child and man
arcs up in a complex maneuver
of such stunning grace
even the Marco Polos are silenced

surfacing to an admiring retinue
of girls' eyes that turn as he passes
they call for him to do it again
to do it again and he obliges
over and over

until the concession stand closes
and chairs are being stacked away
then he mounts the board one last time
drawing out an enormous spring
that shoots him straight up
free style

arms and legs akimbo
dark hair flying
rising to an incredible height
on the joy that works the body

rising and rising
to hang incandescent
suspended for a moment
against the evening's darkening blue

still master of his destiny
still held in that sweet limbo of youth
before the long relentless descent
through the ever deepening waters
of time

summer

is lying down naked
on top of cool clean sheets
beneath the whir of the paddle fan
knowing that tomorrow
the sun is supposed to shine all day
and you have no commitments

night music

awake after midnight
I hear the pulse of traffic
from the turnpike trucks
later a train whistles past
the Church Street crossing
pulling me down the empty tracks
and out into the dark

closing my eyes again
I can see all those travelers
people I will never know
going places I will never be
all those tiny parallel worlds
that coexist yet never overlap

I drift out further
on the music of the night
the foghorn sounding near the point
is not enough to save me
almost lost
you turn over and sigh
and the slow steady rhythm
of your sleeping breath
pulls me back
holding fast as any anchor
here inside the small warm universe
of our own creation

outside
the travelers rush on
beyond our knowledge of the morning
passing over the horizon
and out towards the dark matter
that fills the space around the stars

ABOUT THE AUTHOR

Margot Lavoie, a native of Syracuse, New York, has lived in Wisconsin, Pennsylvania and, briefly, in Oklahoma. Currently she lives in Prairie Grove, Arkansas with her husband Tom. She earns her living working as a medical records coder. She lives through writing, music and the support of a wonderful circle of family and friends.

ACKNOWLEDGMENTS

Grateful acknowledgment is made to the following publications, in which these poems have appeared.

> *Northeast Corridor:* "seeing the city"; *Poesia:* "watching my son as he draws"; *Red Owl:* "night music"; *the Seasons:* "chinook"

Many thanks to Mendy Knott and Leigh Wilkerson for their interest in this project, and to Liz Lester for her lovely and skillful book design. Special thanks to Ginny Masullo for creating such a beautiful evocative painting for the cover. And, to honor the memory of dear friends and those who cared for them with such compassion and grace, all royalties from the sale of this book will be donated to local hospice organizations.

—M. L.

Printed in the United States
222158BV00002B/4/P